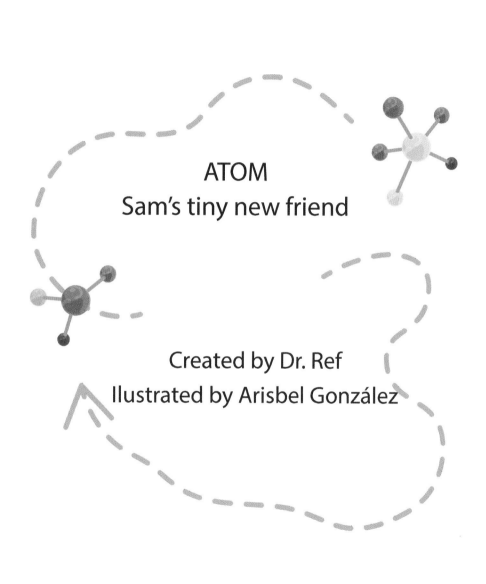

ATOM
Sam's tiny new friend

Created by Dr. Ref
Ilustrated by Arisbel González

Hello!
My name is Sam.
I love to play outside.

I am collecting stones of different sizes.
Search with me.

I filled my basket with stones.
Now I am going to stack them.

I place my stones on top of each other.
Starting with the largest and ending with the tiniest.

Gently, I place the smallest one on top.
It's so small!
I think I found the smallest thing
in the whole world!

Suddenly I hear a voice saying :
I am an ATOM
I am the smallest object.

I am smaller
than an ant.

I am even smaller
than a pea.

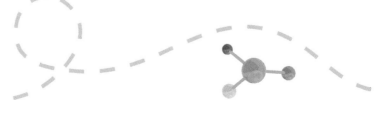

You can't see me because
I am too small to be seen.

But don't worry, I am not alone,
I have many friends!

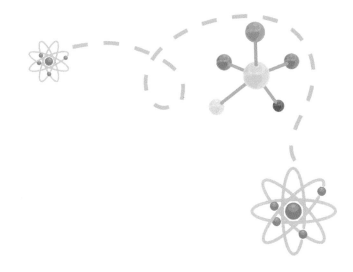

My friends, the other atoms, and I
form small teams,
called Molecules.

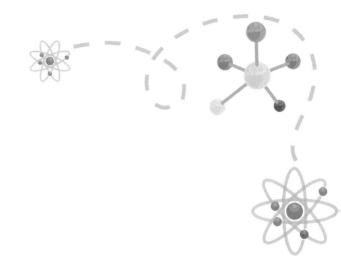

Everything is made of Molecules.

Everything you eat and drink
is made up of molecules.

Cheese

Apple

Sandwich

Milk

Juice

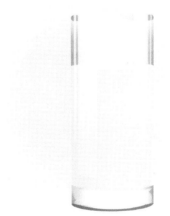

Water

We also make up all the objects.

We make up books,

and chairs.

We are also in nature.

We make up the sand,

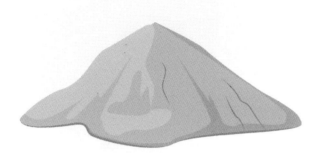

and the beautiful flower.

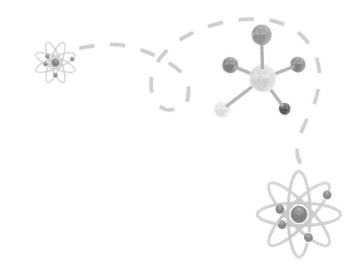

An ATOM is tiny.

You can't see it, but an ATOM can
be found everywhere.

ATOM

Printed in Great Britain
by Amazon